Day Trading for Beginners

The Day Trading Guide for Making Money with Stocks, Options, Forex and More

Table of Contents

Introduction

I want to thank you and commend you for downloading the book, "Day Trading: The Day Trading Guide for Making Money with Stocks, Options, Forex and More."

This book will introduce you to day trading, starting with the important question, is it right for you? If it is, this book will tell you how to get started, how to make money, how to avoid losing money, and a lot of the technical information you'll need.

Thanks again for downloading this book, I hope you enjoy it!

1. Is Day Trading Right for You?

When J.P. Morgan was asked what the market would do that day, he said, "It will fluctuate."

"Day trading" means buying and selling stocks so that you close out all trades at the end of the day. When the market closes in the evening, you no longer own any of the stocks you've been trading, and hopefully, you've made some money on your trades. With discipline and knowledge, you can make quite a bit of money day trading – and enjoy doing it, too.

You need to understand that day trading is not investment. It is also not gambling. It's speculation, and here's the difference: a roulette wheel at the casino is purely random. Even if you don't know the exact odds on every kind of bet, you can be sure that the casino does. A few people will make a lot of money and most people (except for the ones who own the casino!) will lose money, and it's completely unpredictable which group is which. On the other hand, putting money into a bank savings account is as close to a sure deal as you will ever get in this uncertain world. It's also a rock-solid certainty that you won't make very much money that way.

Investing in the stock market means studying individual companies to determine their real value, and putting money into those that have a good future ahead. If you do this conscientiously, you will almost certainly make money... but there's a bit of randomness in this, and sometimes all the care you can give won't be enough to avoid losing some money.

Playing poker follows this rule: you can't win without both luck and skill, but you can always lose by playing badly. That is, the hand that a poker player draws is determined by pure luck, but what he does with his luck depends on skill.

Day trading has more risk than investing, but also can yield better returns. It depends less on luck than poker, usually pays better, and you don't have to keep that stiff "poker face"!

If the charts only contain random wavy lines, then day trading would be gambling. If you knew exactly where the price of a stock was going, it would be a sure thing (hint: forget it!).

The fluctuations in daily stock prices are almost-but-not-quite random, and it's that little edge of predictability that will allow you to make a profit in day trading. No day trader makes a profit every day, but with knowledge and discipline, you can come out ahead often, better than most people can do by investing and much more controllable than gambling.

2. What Do You Need to Be a Day Trader?

First and most importantly, you need to be the kind of person who can learn from study, who can make decisions based on rational thinking and not emotions, who can make a plan and follow it, who can lose money without getting upset and make money without getting giddy, and who has at least a couple of hours in the mornings and in the afternoons which can be devoted to day trading with no interruptions.

Next, you need some money you can afford to lose. If you can't afford to lose any money, or you get anxious whenever you do, this activity is not for you.

You need a direct electronic account with a brokerage that offers support for day traders (see the next section).

You should have a fairly new computer with a reliable, fast Internet connection. Here's a tip: if you are using a laptop on your home wi-fi, run a cable from the router directly to your computer's ethernet port and connect that way instead. It will be faster and more secure. Trying to trade on a non-secured wi-fi network is just asking for trouble, so don't try to pursue this career at the coffee shop. It's very handy to add a second monitor if your computer will support this.

Finally, you need time to learn and study before you launch into day trading. Spend enough time doing fictional, practice trades that you can be confident of your decisions before you trade for real.

3. How to Set Up a Brokerage Account

As a day trader, you will need an on-line trading account so that you can execute your own trades. Traditional brokerages let you call your broker, get advice from him or her, and buy or sell stocks. This is often extremely helpful. But a day trader might be executing orders every few minutes, which your broker can't handle, and you also must get the lower fees associated with doing your own trades, or you won't make a profit.

Here's a good list of brokerages that will set up a day-trading account for you: https://www.nerdwallet.com/blog/investing/best-online-brokers-for-stock-trading/

Here's what you should look for in choosing a brokerage:

- Price. Since you will be trading all the time, you need a low price for each trade. But be cautious here: brokers have, to use some technical terminology, a whole boatload of ways to charge you money, and a broker with low per-trade fees might turn out to be very expensive. Fees can include account maintenance fees, account inactivity fees, charges for telephone calls, and even more creative tricks.

- Minimum starting balance. You need to put some money into the account, and be prepared to say goodbye to it. That is (to repeat): don't put any money into a brokerage account that you can't afford to lose.

- Trading platform. This means the software you will use for trading, which might be an application you download to your computer (in which case, be sure it runs on your system), or a program that runs on the brokerage's server, which you will reach using your internet browser. Try this software out before making a commitment. If it seems confusing or slow, you may want to shop around for another brokerage.

- Brokerage services. A brokerage that is set up for traditional investors can provide invaluable research about stocks. As a day trader, you're not looking for the same qualities as a long-term investor, but if you don't mind paying for the information, it can still be very useful to you.

4. Some Things to Know First

We'll start out, in this book, discussing day trading in the stock market. Other markets are also good for day trading, and are discussed later.

A **candlestick graph** represents the price changes to a stock over some period of time, which might be a day, an hour or part of an hour. This technique, interestingly enough, was actually developed in the 18th century in Japan to describe the price of rice, which explains the Japanese terminology.

This book will discuss stock prices by talking about the candlestick graph because it's a very common graph type, and conveys quite a bit of useful information. On a candlestick graph, the lines at the top and bottom (which are called "shadows") mark off the highest and lowest prices for that stock during the period covered (which might be as short as a minute). The candle body is dark if the price is going down – that is, if the closing price was less than the opening price. The body is light if the price is going up. If the stock comes back to about the same place it started, you get a cross called a "doji". If the price didn't move at all, the candlestick graph is just a horizontal line with no shadows.

A **long sale** is what you probably think of as normal: you buy stock when the price is low and you expect it to go up. If it does, you sell the stock at a profit. A **short sale** is a way to make money if you expect the price to go down. In a short sale, the broker loans you some shares of stock so that you can sell them, even though you don't own them. During the day, you'll have to buy enough shares to pay back the broker. If the price does go down, then you can buy the shares for less than you sold them for, and you make a profit. If the price goes up, you made the wrong decision. You still have to buy that stock to give it back to the broker, but now you'll have to pay even more for it.

Using both techniques, a day trader who makes correct predictions can profit from any movement in price, up or down.

A **stop-loss order** is a vital tool you must use to limit the amount you can lose on a bad purchase of stock. You set a stop-loss for whatever amount of loss you can tolerate, based on the price of the stock or a percentage change. If the stock price goes down below the stop-loss price, your broker will sell it automatically. No one likes to lose money, but a stop-loss will protect you from losing more than you want to. The stop-loss point is not a mathematical decision, it's based on your financial situation and your personality: it represents how much you are willing to lose before you call it quits.

Liquidity means how easily you can buy or sell a stock. An "illiquid" stock has only a few people trading it, which can be a problem: you can't buy if no one is selling or sell if no one is buying. For day trading, you want highly liquid stocks.

Volatility refers to how much the stock price moves up or down in a day. If the price doesn't move much, a day trader can't make money on it. On the other hand, a stock with too much volatility (that is, the price swings wildly) probably means that a lot of traders are reacting to rumors or irrational fears, and a careful day trader will want to stay out of that market.

Slippage is the amount of price movement that happens between the time you place an order and the time the order is executed. Slippage is always bad and you want to minimize it. It depends on the kind of trading software you use, the speed of your internet connection, the volatility of the stock, the current load on your broker, and the overall activity level of the market.

5. Trading Patterns and Strategies

When you study a stock price's daily movements long enough, you will see patterns that emerge, and strategies for buying and selling that would be profitable. This list describes some of the patterns that day traders look for, and strategies they use.

The interesting thing about these patterns is that every one of them works... some of the time. Every one of them will also fail, some of the time. If there were a guaranteed strategy that always worked, of course everybody would use it. But nothing in the world actually works that way, and it's emphatically not true for day trading.

Here's what does work: every day trader develops his own strategy, using a mixture of patterns that are unique. No two day traders will operate exactly the same way. This means, first, that you can come up with a strategy that will work for you, and second, that you (like every day trader) will be a pioneer trying something that no one else has done. That's part of what makes it fun!

One last caveat, which is so obvious that it's easy to overlook: if you think it's the right time to buy stock, necessarily somebody else thinks it's the right time to sell. You can't sell stock unless somebody else wants to

---

buy it. In every transaction, one side is right and the other side is wrong. Your edge is your experience, your constant attention, and your disciplined adherence to a strategy.

News Trading

The stock market is twitchy about news. Every financial story that appears on TV, and many of the non-financial news stories, will send some stocks up and some down. For example, you hear that a pipeline has burst in Kansas. This is obviously bad news for the pipeline company, for the oil companies that ship on that pipeline, for any business in a town that might be affected by the physical oil, for wheat farmers whose crops may be spoiled, for food companies that buy wheat or for any oil company that has a pending application to build a pipeline anywhere else in America. It's good news for spill-remediation companies or food companies that use some other grain. It might be good or bad for truckers, who might get tanker business while the pipeline is being repaired, but who also might have to pay higher gas prices. It might be good or bad for organic-food companies, pipeline control and instrumentation companies, or alternative energy companies.

How can you tell which stocks will rise and which will fall? You need experience and expertise in some particular sub-set of the market. No one can keep track of all of the effects of a news story, but you can get an edge by understanding one little corner of the market.

It's important to understand that as a day trader, you really aren't concerned with what a news story *actually* means for companies. Because you are trading on a time horizon of hours or less, you are only trying to gauge the immediate reactions of other traders and investors. You are trying to anticipate how *they* will feel about this story. In other words, this is a problem in psychology more than a problem in economics.

You will need to keep a continuous eye on news from multiple sources to use this strategy. Professional traders tend to work in a sea of monitors showing financial and business news from sources such as CNN or Bloomberg.

Trending

Trending is also called momentum trading. This the simplest pattern, and simplicity can be a good thing! It just means seeing which way the price seems to be going, and assuming it will keep going that way for a while. The reason you make this assumption is that you've watched this stock, and noticed that that's the way the price seems to move.

Trend day trading is about watching the price graph, not about second-guessing why a stock is moving or who is buying and selling. Your goal here is to identify when a stock starts moving in one direction, based on similar movements you've watched in the past. Any trend movement will stop and reverse after a while, and it's up to you to have a sense of when that will be so that you can get out on time.

Don't neglect to have a stop-loss order on every stock you trade by trends.

Scalping

A "scalper" makes money by executing a lot of very quick, very small trades. He buys a stock and sells it, often only a few minutes later, when it has gone up a few cents. He shorts a stock and buys when the price has gone down a few cents.

Repeat this pattern a hundred or more times in a day, and you can make a good total profit by the end of the day. (This strategy depends crucially on getting a very cheap price for each trade from your broker.) Because you need to buy and sell fairly large blocks of stock to make a significant profit, however, this strategy increases your risk of loss.

Contrarian Trading

Sarah Palin had a scornful proverb for those who follow trends: "Only dead fish go with the flow." Stocks always go up after a down-trend and down after an up-trend. Clearly, if you bet against the trend, you're bound to be right some of the time, and you get the satisfaction of telling yourself you're not just part of the crowd.

However, you don't need to be very smart just to see which way the parade is going and march the other way. A successful contrarian doesn't need or make use of an opinion on which way the whole market is going. Instead, a contrarian looks for an unloved stock that, for some irrational reason, is trading below its true value, or for a stock that has been over-hyped so that it is priced higher than the company is really worth. In either situation, the trend is bound to reverse, and the contrarian wants to get there before everybody else figures this out.

A day-trading contrarian faces a slightly different problem. Since you want to close out all transactions before the end of the day, you will need to look for irrational price movements that go up and down within hours.

Sometimes this happens because of news. Example: X Company announces a management reorganization, and the stock price goes down. You get your advantage by knowing something about X Company. If you think that other investors are just being hysterical and the management re-org was needed and will make the company stronger, then you should watch the price go down until the stock is clearly undervalued, then buy. If the market comes to its senses before the end of the day, the price will go back up by the time you sell.

An opposite example: Y Drugs announces tests of a new drug to cure Creeping Crud (or something). The market goes crazy and the price spikes. By understanding the news better than most, you know that Y Drugs is several years away from having a marketable product, so you short the stock when it is high enough to be clearly overvalued.

Sometimes an irrational price can occur because of movements of the whole market – that is, the Dow Jones average (or some other collective indicator of your choice) goes up or down, and takes stocks with it that are really not affected by whatever elation or depression has caused the investors to move. If you believe the correction will come during the day for those particular stocks, you can place a contrary order and make a profit.

Intuitive Trading

Here's a swell fifty-cent word for you: *pareidolia* (par-i-DOL-ee-ah). It's the reason why people see faces in things that don't actually have faces, such as the "Man in the Moon", the tail ends of cars, or toast with splotchy burns. It means the human tendency to want to make meaningful patterns out of the data we see, even if the data is random.

This is also the reason why every slot-machine player in Las Vegas has a theory that predicts when a slot machine is going to pay off, such as "after you've lost twenty times in a row" or "when you get two cherries with another cherry only one space away" or "in the early morning when not many people are playing". Of course all of these theories are worthless, since slot machines pay off at random.

But pareidolia is related to the deeply human ability to extract *real* patterns when they aren't obvious. People are much better at doing this than computers, because it's an evolutionary skill that was important to our distant ancestors.

For example, if you watch a lot of movies, you may have the ability to look at a character in the first ten minutes and say, "That guy's going to get killed before the end." You can do this even if you can't say why you think that, because your brain is processing many subtle signals that are below the level of consciousness.

An "intuitive" day-trader can develop a gut-instinct about how the market will move, after a learning period that might require years. If you have this ability, it's quite legitimate to use it in trading, and can be very profitable. Intuitive traders often say they are following a strategy even when they really aren't, because they're afraid they will look silly if they say they're following a hunch.

However, this is an extremely tricky strategy and it's very easy to fool yourself – and lose a lot of money! A valid hunch is different from an emotional reaction, or the desire to follow the crowd or to go the other way from the crowd, or the desire to look smarter than you are, or dozens of other psychological tricks your brain can play on you.

A good intuitive trader absorbs vast amounts of information, studies the price charts and avoids committing to "theories" that aren't real. Instead, an intuitive trader tests his gut instinct against data. If your hunches tend to be good, it's okay to follow them.

But if you (like most people) are not naturally and correctly intuitive, you should develop a strategy and stick to it, without making sudden impulsive buys or sales.

Price Action Trading

A "price-action" trader looks at short-term candlestick patterns rather than the overall movement of a stock price.

The harami pattern involves two candlesticks next to each other, of different colors. The first has a long body, and the second has a short body entirely within the limits of the longer body.

What the **harami** means, to a price-action trader, is that a trend has just run out its course and is starting to reverse. If the first, longer candlestick is black (meaning prices are going down, pretty fast) and the next candlestick is white (meaning prices are going up, but tentatively), that indicates that the down-trend may be over.

If the opposite occurs, and the first candlestick indicates an up-trend and the second indicates a tentative downward movement, then the up-trend may be about to change.

The harami is particularly significant if the two candlesticks represent the closing price one day and the opening price the next day.

The **harami-cross** pattern is the same as the harami, except that the second candlestick is a doji or cross, which indicates that the price movement of the first candlestick has stopped, and now the price is hardly moving at all. The harami-cross pattern is a stronger version of the harami, which indicates that the previous price movement has completely "run out of steam". This probably means the direction is about to reverse.

Engulfing is a pattern that means sentiment about a stock has just shifted abruptly. The picture shows the engulfing pattern between the close of trading one day and the opening the next morning.

The bearish engulfing tells this story: the stock was going up yesterday at the close, and this morning's opening price was up even higher. But then the price went down so far that it closed well below yesterday's lowest price. This means that the "bears" feel pretty strongly that the stock was overvalued, and the price is likely to go down even more.

The bullish engulfing is the opposite story. Even though this stock was going down yesterday, and today opened even lower, some traders believe so much in this stock that they have driven the price above yesterday's best. If they believe the stock is worth more, other traders probably will also, and the price will keep going up.

The **dragonfly** doji (you can see the Japanese influence here!) is a cross doji with a long lower shadow and little or no top shadow. It tells this story: the bears tried to push the price down but were ultimately unsuccessful, because the open, high and close prices are all the same. This may tell you (if confirmed by your other information) that there is quite a bit of support for this stock and the price is likely to go up.

The **gravestone** doji is just the opposite.

Channel or Range Trading

You've probably noticed in your own life that some prices bring emotional reactions. If you're going out to lunch, $12 seems way too high (even though paying that much for supper doesn't seem unreasonable), but lunch for $4 makes you think the food's probably terrible. (Your particular inflection points will vary, of course.)

Many stocks seem to have emotional barriers at the high end (meaning that many traders get the idea the stock has gone too high) and the low end. You can identify this pattern by looking for sharp reversals in the price line, with a repeating pattern over several days.

A channel trader buys when the price goes below the "channel" (often by setting an automatic "buy" order) and sells when the price goes back up. In the same way, a channel trader sells short when the price goes above the channel.

Fibonacci Ratios

This trading pattern is range trading with some special numbers.

If you're the kind of person who thinks math is fun (which is a good mental habit for traders), then you've no doubt met the Fibonacci numbers, a remarkable sequence that mathematicians always enjoy. If you haven't met them, try: https://www.mathsisfun.com/numbers/fibonacci-sequence.html, but note that you don't really need to know all this stuff for the purpose of trading.

What you will be concerned with as a trader is several "magic" ratios. We won't explain here where these numbers come from, but you will need to be familiar with these ratios:

$$61.8\%, 38.2\%, 23.6\%$$

There are two reasons why the Fibonacci ratios are important. First, they show up over and over again in nature. These ratios are found in the spiral shells of snails, in the arrangement of flower petals around the center, in population growth, in probability theory, in pine cones – for whatever reason, the Fibonacci ratios are deeply embedded in the living and non-living world.

More directly related to trading, the Fibonacci ratios also seem to be baked into the human soul. The "Golden Ratio" is 0.618 to 1, and rectangles of this shape have been used by architects and artists for thousands of years. The Parthenon in Greece is famously based on the Golden Ratio, with the same ratio controlling the overall width and height of the building, the relationship between the ground and the lintel, and the lintel and the roof ... and many more. Researchers have tried showing pictures of various buildings and shapes to people who have never heard of the Fibonacci ratios, and consistently, people say that shapes based on that ratio "just look nicer" than shapes that are not. For some reason, people appear to be born with a feeling for the Fibonacci ratios.

And by the way, handsome men and pretty women tend to have ratios between their facial features, such as the distance from mouth to eyes and mouth to nose, that are about that 61.8% point. Hope that's you! (If not, you should learn day trading and make a lot of money, which makes anybody more attractive, right?)

Another study found that people tend to get anxious or sad when they spend more than 61.8% of the money in their wallets. This leads directly to the theory of Fibonacci ratios in trading:

> *People tend to have an emotional reaction when prices, after a trend, move to positions that correspond to the Fibonacci ratios.*

If this sounds flaky to you, consider that while it may not be real, the market is full of traders who have read books like this, and *they* think it's real, which means that this is something of a self-fulfilling prophecy.

This theory is so common that trading-graphics software often includes a tool to draw the Fibonacci ratios automatically.

6. Trading on Margin

"Margin" is the term traders use for borrowing money to make trades. The amount of margin a trader can get depends on the amount of money he has in his brokerage account, and also on his history with that broker.

A trader with margin can buy stock with, say, 30% of his own money and 70% borrowed from the broker, which lets him buy and sell much larger blocks of stock than he could do on his own. If he trades successfully, he makes that much more money on each share. He can pay back the broker and keep a larger profit, often many hundreds of times larger.

Here's the rule on margin trading:

> *Many day traders can make more money by trading on margin.*
>
> *However, not you.*
>
> *Yes, seriously.*

The reason why you can't successfully trade on margin is because you are reading this book, which is aimed at introducing beginners to the world of day trading. If you knew enough about trading to handle a margin account, you wouldn't be here.

Margin trading offers much higher rewards at a much higher risk. You can make or lose fortunes in the course of a single day. Debt is often called "leverage" because you use only a small amount of your own money to swing very large trades. Here's what you need to know about leverage: leverage let's you control a big swing with a small effort. But of course, it works both ways!

So the rule is, when you have enough experience to be able to trade with leverage (and probably long after you've forgotten about reading this not-really-joking joke), your broker will offer you a margin account. Until then, it's not for you.

7. Day Trading in Options

Like many things, you have to buy an "option" for money. What you have bought is a contract that gives you the right to either buy some stock at a fixed price within a time limit (a "call") or the right to sell some stock at a fixed price within a time limit (a "put").

You can either buy or sell options.

An option is optional for you, as the buyer – you don't have to use it if you don't want to. This saves you from having to do a trade that will cost you money, but then you will have spent the price you paid for the option for nothing.

But when you are the buyer, an option is not at all optional for the seller. If you have bought the right to buy stock at the set price, the seller *must* sell it to you at that price, even if he doesn't want to – and of course he would prefer not to sell, because the only reason you want to buy that stock is that it's worth more now than you will pay. If you have bought the right to sell stock, the buyer *has* to buy it even though the only reason you're selling is because the price has gone down and you can sell it for more.

Here's a table that summarizes how options work for the buyer:

You bought a ...	Price Rises	Price Falls	Option Expires
PUT option	You would be sad if you had to exercise this option, because you'd have to sell the stock at the agreed price, even though it's selling for more now. Fortunately, you don't have to do this.	*You're happy!* You get to sell a block of stock at the agreed price, but you can buy it right now for less than that, so you make money on the difference.	*You're annoyed but also relieved.* You bought an option you didn't use, so you wasted the price of the option. On the other hand, you didn't lose any more than that.
CALL option	*You're happy!* You can buy the stock at the agreed price, which is less than the current price. You could sell that stock immediately, and make money on the difference.	You would be sad if you had to exercise this option, because you'd have to buy the stock for the agreed price even though it's not worth that much now. Fortunately, you don't have to do this.	

You can be a buyer or seller of put options, or a buyer or seller of call options. If you buy an option, some other trader sold it to you. One of you thinks the price will go up, the other thinks the price will go down. Obviously, you can't both be right.

If you decide not to exercise an option you buy (because you'd lose money on the deal), you do nothing, and the option time expires. In this case, the seller makes a little money because he keeps the option price, and you lose the same amount.

Options are what is called a zero-sum game: if the buyer makes money, the seller loses money, and vice-versa. Options are popular because they let a trader optimize his risk to any level he's comfortable with, as we will explain below. The more risk, of course, the more potential profit and also the more potential loss. But if you don't like risk, options also offer some extremely conservative strategies that will let you make a small amount of money with very little risk.

Options are traded using an option account, which is often another service offered by the same brokerage where you trade other securities. Most often, you will be required to keep a certain amount of money in your account.

Options Terminology

For some reason, the options market has a lot of odd-sounding terminology, with acronyms, and often multiple phrases that mean the same thing.

Strike Price – the price that was set on an option. This is the price at which the option holder can buy (for a call option) or sell (for a put option).

In the Money – this means that the current stock price is over the strike price for a call or under the strike price for a put option. In other words, this is the point at which the option holder can make a profit. Related terms with acronyms:

- In the Money (ITM) – the current price is better than the strike price.

- Out of the Money (OTM) – the current price is worse than the strike price.

- At the Money (ATM) – the current price and the strike price are about the same.

It's important to note that ITM and OTM do not necessarily indicate that an option is profitable, because there are some other factors to consider. These terms really just indicate the relationship between the current and strike prices.

The "Covered Call": A Conservative Strategy

The "covered call" is not a day-trading strategy, but it is a very useful technique for any trader and it illustrates a number of ideas about options that we will use later. In a covered call, you sell a call option, with a strike price that is higher than the current price, against a block of stock which you already own, and which you are thinking of selling anyway. This strategy is as conservative as any trade can be: you can almost certainly make a little money, with very little risk. Most likely, the worst that can happen is that you won't make as much money as you could have.

Here's how it works: let's say you already own 100 shares of Amalgamated Treeshade, which is currently selling for $100 a share. You're thinking of unloading this, but you don't have to make any immediate moves. So you go to the options market and sell a call with a strike price of $110 per share and a time limit of three months. In other words, you have sold some other trader the right to buy your shares for $110 each, anytime over the next three months. You sell this right for, let's say, 85 cents a share or $85 total.

The $85 dollars is yours to keep in any event. You can put that in your pocket and go out to spend it on a very nice dinner for two.

For the buyer, this call option is a pretty good deal. Three months is a long time, and the buyer knows that the price has been over $110 before, so it's a fairly good bet that sometime during the life of this option, the price is going to go above $110 per share. When that happens, the buyer will exercise his option and make you sell him that stock. Let's say the price has gone up to $115 per share. The buyer can turn around and sell that stock, and keep five dollars per share. He's just made $500, less the $85 he had to pay you for that option.

If you are a smart trader, you say "I feel good. I just sold my stock for $10 a share more than it was worth when I sold that option, so I made a thousand bucks, plus a dinner at a swell restaurant."

If you are a foolish and emotional trader, you smack yourself hard on the forehead and cry, "What a fool I was! If I hadn't sold that option, I could have sold that stock for $15 a share more, and made another five hundred dollars." If you're that kind of trader, (1) you will go broke fairly shortly, because you lack the emotional stability you need for trading, (2) you will be unhappy most of the time you're still trading, and (3) your forehead is going to hurt.

If the stock price never does go above $110, then when the option expires you still have your stock and you still have the $85 from the sale of the option. You can go out and sell another option against the same block of stock. The buyer of that option misses his $85 but isn't otherwise hurt.

But think about that time period of 3 months. When the option is fresh, three months gives plenty of time for the stock price to move, so that option is worth $85. As days pass, it becomes less and less likely that the option is going to go ITM (In The Money) in the remaining time. When it gets to the point that the option expires tomorrow, it's worth only a few pennies at best, because only an incurable optimist is going to believe the stock price will move ITM overnight.

Options are contracts which can be bought and sold like any other asset. As a covered-call investor, you don't care what the current value of your call option is because you've already gotten the money for it.

But if you are a day-trader in options, you may be interested in buying that call option or selling it to someone else. To make this point more strongly, there's almost no market for one-day puts and calls. A day trader in options is buying and selling options that still have some time before they expire.

Here's what you need to know about day-trading in options:

1. Time is Money. Options usually are worth most when they are fresh, and lose value steadily after that. But there are very profitable exceptions if the underlying value of the stock moves so that the option begins to look like a better bet.

2. A day trader rarely holds on to an option long enough to exercise it. Instead, you buy or sell options to other traders. At some point, either the option is worth exercising (this is said to have "intrinsic value") or it times-out and is worth nothing. An option that has intrinsic value may still be worth selling rather than cashing in – you might be able to sell it to someone who believes it will gain even more intrinsic value.

Is Options Trading for You?

Buying and selling options over a longer time horizon than a day offers a whole range of patterns from very conservative (such as the covered-call option described above) to very risky. As always, the more risk you take, the greater the potential reward and also the greater the potential loss.

Day-trading in options is a little different. It is a kind of trading you can do without much capital, and it offers the chance of very good returns. But it requires a tremendous study of various strategies and patterns, more than can be covered in this book, to account for all the factors that make options more or less valuable. These include:

- The time to expiry and the cost of the option.

- The relationship of the strike price to the current stock price.

- The particular prospects of the company whose stock is optioned.

- The mood of the market.

- Technical price-action patterns similar to those discussed above for stock trading.

If you are willing to invest the time and study, and to accept inevitable losses, then day-trading in options may be a money maker for you!

8. Day Trading on the Foreign Exchange Market

Everybody likes to have United States dollars, but they're not legal currency anywhere except in the United States. $US are theoretically not good anywhere else.

As a practical matter, though, people all over the world will sell you stuff for $US, because they have faith that they can sell those $US dollars to somebody who will pay for them in whatever local currency they actually do use.

The definition of "money" is anything at all that you can exchange for stuff or services. Anybody in another country who has $US believes that eventually those dollars will get back to America and be valuable to somebody who wants to buy something for them. In the meantime, they're valuable as money because the person who holds them can exchange them for stuff or services, wherever they are.

The market in the middle that allows people to exchange one currency for another is called Foreign Exchange or Forex.

The price of money goes up or down just like anything else that can be bought or sold. Here's an example with the fictitious country of "Elbonia" (with apologies the cartoonist Scott Adams). In Elbonia, the money is goats. If you're going to visit Elbonia (not recommended!), the Elbonian bank will exchange your $US in this ratio at, say, 9:00 AM on a particular morning:

You'll get 3.16 Elbonian Goats for each US dollar you have. (How can you have 0.16 of a Goat? The answer is too technical to present here. Trust us.)

However, that price changes every few minutes, depending on how many people want to exchange their money for Elbonian Goats. If there are lots of tourists coming to Elbonia (why?), the bank might find that by the afternoon, it only has to offer 2.86 Goats to get one dollar. To put this another way, there are a lot of dollars chasing the Elbonian currency, so each dollar is worth less in that exchange. This has no effect on the value of the $US in the United States, which continues to be what it always was.

On the other hand, if the truth about how Elbonian food tastes gets out to the tourists, they'll leave. The bank might have to offer 4.23 Goats per dollar in the afternoon. That is, the bank has to pay more in Goats to get a dollar.

That evening, you cash in your Goats for $US. If the price of dollars went up (a trader gets more Goats per dollar), then your Goats are not worth as much and you wind up with fewer $US than you had when you started. If the price of dollars went down (a trader gets fewer Goats for one dollar), then your Goats will be worth more dollars and you will have made some money.

The Foreign Exchange Market

The Foreign Exchange market (Forex) is completely decentralized. Unlike stocks, which are traded on only a few exchanges, the Forex market is known as an "over-the-counter" market and takes place all over the world. Much of it is inter-bank exchanges that nobody else ever sees. Moreover, because there are so many venues for exchanging currencies, there is typically not one exchange rate between two currencies, but a range of rates depending on where you make the exchange.

Forex runs 24 hours a day during the week, but is not active on weekends. It is the most liquid market there is. During the hours it is open, you can exchange any currency for any other at any time.

Currencies are always traded in pairs, such as $US and Euros, or Australian Dollars and Yuan (the currency of China). In each case, each currency has a price expressed in the other currency. An example might be EUR/USD (Euros to US Dollars) 1.3519 bid and 1.3525 ask. The **bid** price is what you will get if you sell either currency, and the **ask** price is what you will pay to buy that currency.

Note that your Forex broker does not charge a fee or commission for transactions. Instead, the broker gets its income from the **spread** between the bid and ask prices.

Profits and losses in Forex transactions are measured in **pips**, where a pip is 0.0001 of the value of a currency – in other words, one one-hundredth of one percent. (Exception: for the Japanese Yen, one pip is defined as 1%.) A **block** of currency is 100,000 single bills of that kind of money, and is the basic unit of Forex trading. (However, your broker will probably offer "mini" and "micro" blocks that will let you trade much smaller amounts.)

Example: Suppose you are trading Canadian Dollars against US Dollars and CAN/USD changes from 1.0345 to 1.0350. If you are holding Canadian Dollars, you can sell them for US Dollars and make 5 pips per Canadian Dollar. If you are trading one block, then your profit in US Dollars is:

100,000 X 0.0005 = 5. You just made 5 bucks American!

The value of a pip changes every moment, until you complete a transaction and buy or sell your block of currency.

Forex trading is almost always done on **margin**. You put a certain amount of money into your account with the broker, and the broker extends margin to you so that you can buy or sell much larger volumes of currency. Your broker will specify how much actual cash you need to put in to get started – as always, this must be money you can afford to lose. Note that if you lose money and your account runs dry, your ability to trade stops at that moment, even if you are in the middle of a transaction.

A Forex **robot** is a computer program you can run on some trading platforms that will execute trades for you. Naturally, every seller of robots will say their product is a guaranteed profit maker and just as naturally, you won't believe them. However, a robot chosen after diligent research (which means that you understand what the robot is doing and why) may be a good choice for you.

Why Exchange Rates Vary

What makes the Forex market volatile is that many, many factors affect currency exchange rates. These include the underlying strength of a country's economy, the available of credit for a country on the world market, the general state of the world economy and the export/import balance of a country.

In addition, currency trading is subject to the same kinds of news, rumors, and gossip that make all other financial markets wiggly.

All of this is to say, your constant study and attention will be necessary to prosper in this market.

Day Trading Forex

Despite being done on margin, day trading Forex can be a fairly safe and conservative activity. Most day traders follow strategies that are similar to those used for stock trading. In particular, Forex day traders often use the trend follower, scalping, and price action strategies.

If you are cautious about creating a rational trading strategy and sticking to it, without "bailing out" prematurely when you get nervous about losing money and without staying longer than your strategy suggests when you are winning, then you can make a good income day trading in the foreign exchange market.

Conclusion

I hope this book was able to help you to understand how day-trading works with various kinds of financial products, and how you can make a profit by trading.

The next step is to find an exchange that will let you set up a practice account, which will let you buy and sell with play money. Keep notes of what works and what doesn't as you practice trading. At the same time, study, study, study! Study more about how day-trading works, study about the companies whose stock you want to trade. Try to develop your own strategy for trading, and change it until you get something that works.

Then you can start trading with real money.

If you have enjoyed this book, please be sure to leave a review and a comment to let us know how we are doing so we can continue to bring you quality ebooks.

Thank you and good luck!

www.ingramcontent.com/pod-product-compliance
Lightning Source LLC
Chambersburg PA
CBHW071831200526
45169CB00018B/1340